WHY SHOULD I CARE ABOUT THE ANCIENT GREEKS?

By Don Nardo

Consultant
Robert. B. Kebric, Ph.D.
Senior Professor of History (Retired)
University of Louisville
Louisville, KY

COMPASS POINT BOOKS
a capstone imprint

Why Should I Care About History? is published by Compass Point Books, an imprint of Capstone.
1710 Roe Crest Drive, North Mankato, Minnesota 56003
www.capstonepub.com

Library of Congress Cataloging-in-Publication Data is available on the Library of Congress website.
ISBN: 978-0-7565-6422-3 (library binding)
ISBN: 978-0-7565-6565-7 (paperback)
ISBN: 978-0-7565-6423-0 (eBook PDF)

Summary: Every four years, the world celebrates one of the most exciting contributions of the ancient Greeks: the Olympic Games. That, of course, is not all this great civilization left behind. From theater to democracy, discover how the Greeks' ancient inventions and philosophies evolved into objects and ideas we know and treasure today.

Image Credits:
Alamy: AF archive, 59, Eye Ubiquitous, 33, Ivy Close Images, 53, Universal Images Group North America LLC, 31 (top); Newscom: 1492 PICTURES/FOX 2000 PICTURES/IMPRINT ENTERTAINMENT / Album, 58, akg-images, 13, Heritage Images/The Ann Ronan Picture Library, 56, Heritage Images/The Print Collector, 27, Pictures From History/Ohio Statehouse, 18, SportsChrome/Sport the Library, 37, Universal Images Group/De Agostini/A. Dagli Orti, 39, World History Archive, 57; Shutterstock: Aerial-motion, 19, Aleksandar Todorovic, 45, Andronos Haris, 55, Boerescu, 26, Everett Historical, 17, Foto-Migawki MD, 35, Fouad A. Saad, 7, Gilmanshin, 42, Jana Janina, 36, Nasky, 9, Nice Shutterstock, 11, Pit Stock, 46, PNIK, 31 (bottom), Ranta Images, Cover (right), Rob Crandall, 24, Sven Hansche, 22, vangelis aragiannis, Cover (left), Vladimir Korostyshevskiy, 51; XNR Productions, 6

Design Elements:
Shutterstock: Artem Kovalenco

Editorial Credits:
Editor: Gina Kammer; Designer: Tracy McCabe; Media Researcher: Jo Miller; Production Specialist: Laura Manthe

Printed and bound in the United States of America.
PA99

TABLE OF CONTENTS

CHAPTER 1

GOOD THINKING: THE FIRST SCIENTISTS AND PHILOSOPHERS

Did you know that science, democracy, the Olympics, and actors playing roles have one thing in common? They were all invented in ancient Greece. Twenty-four centuries ago, Athens was Greece's leading city-state. The Athenians introduced many cultural advances, such as plays, acting, and theaters. They and other Greeks also made important moves in politics, science, sports, law, and architecture.

These fabulous feats filled the Athenian leader Pericles with pride. "Future ages will wonder at us," he remarked. And with time, that daring prediction came true. People around the world now stand in awe of the ancient Greek achievement. While it's easy to overlook, even your generation owes the Greeks a big cultural debt.

Black Sea

Thrace

Thasos

Macedonia

Mount Olympus ▲

Illyria

Hellespont (Dardanelles)

Epirus

Thessaly

Aegean

Lesbos

ASIA MINOR

Sea

Delphi•

Gulf of Corinth

Olympia• Corinth•

•Athens

Argos•

Peloponnesus

•Sparta

N
W   E
S

Crete

0   90 miles
0   90 kilometers

Mediterranean Sea

Greece is mostly surrounded by the Mediterranean Sea and the Aegean Sea. The mountainous land meant that many ancient Greeks settled along the coast and on the many islands off the coast.

WHO WERE THE ANCIENT GREEKS, ANYWAY?

The Greeks reached their political and cultural height between about 600 and 300 BC. Greece was never a united country in those days. Instead, it was made up of hundreds of city-states. Each was a tiny, independent nation built around a central town. The Greek states were defeated and absorbed by Rome in the last couple centuries BC.

The introduction of steam engines in the 1700s led to the rise of major modern industries. But these were not the first steam engines. The first-century Greek inventor Hero of Alexandria built a small one. To him it was only a toy. He never thought to use it to create large-scale industry.

Hero's small-scale steam engine was called an aeolipile. Boiling water produced steam, which made the central sphere spin.

THE GRANDEST IDEA

Today the entire world operates through various kinds of technology. So science is perhaps the biggest single part of the debt we owe the Greeks. In fact, the world's first scientists appeared in ancient Greece. They were the earliest thinkers to try to explain how nature works. They did this without turning to gods, demons, and magic. This made them different from thinkers in Egypt, Babylonia, and other ancient lands. The Egyptians, for instance, thought that supernatural beings controlled nature. Many Greek citizens believed that too.

But the Greek scientists did not. Instead, they saw the universe as a cosmos. In other words, they defined the universe as an orderly domain that works via natural laws.

This was the single grandest idea they proposed. Namely, everything that exists has a natural, physical cause. And more than that, humans can discover those causes. Through evidence, logic, and experiments, they can learn how nature operates. Science is the process by which all that happens.

WAY OUT THERE! EARLY COSMIC THEORIES

When was the last time you looked up at the stars? You didn't need to wonder what those tiny dots of light were. That's because science has established that they are other suns. They look small and faint because they lie much further away than our own local star. No one knew this, however, before the Greek scientists came along. One, Anaxagoras, was very interested in astronomy. He was far from alone. Numerous early Greek thinkers tried to explain what the sun, planets, and stars were. Anaxagoras was the first known person to correctly call the sun a star. Another Greek scientist, Philolaus, went further. He accurately defined Earth as a planet. Also, like other Greek thinkers, he rejected the notion that Earth is flat. Instead, he said, it is a sphere, like the sun and moon.

These and most other ancient astronomers did make one major error. They pictured Earth at the cosmos's center, or at least near the center. This later became known as the geocentric cosmic model. The highly influential Athenian scholar Plato, born in the late

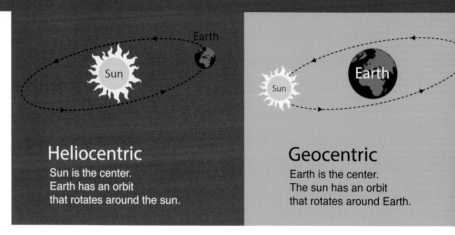

The heliocentric system shows the sun at the center. The geocentric system shows Earth at the center, in which the sun revolved around Earth. The heliocentric version turned out to be the correct one.

Heliocentric
Sun is the center.
Earth has an orbit that rotates around the sun.

Geocentric
Earth is the center.
The sun has an orbit that rotates around Earth.

400s BC, accepted it. So did his brilliant student, Aristotle. Aristotle was widely held in high esteem. In fact, many centuries later, medieval Europeans considered his thinking as flawless. As a result, the geocentric cosmic model remained in place for a long time.

Still, one ancient Greek got Earth's place in the universe correct. His name was Aristarchus of Samos. He concluded that the sun was at the center of things. Earth and the other planets move around it, he said. However, he was unable to compete with Aristotle's towering reputation. So, over time, Aristarchus was largely forgotten. One person who remembered him was Polish astronomer Nicolaus Copernicus. In the 1500s he revived Aristarchus's theory and proved it correct. That marked the birth of modern astronomy.

Maybe you've studied biology in school. If so, you learned about animals and plants and may have dissected a frog in class to examine its body. That is exactly what some of the ancient Greek thinkers did! For example, Aristotle collected and studied hundreds of animal specimens. He also created a complex system of classifying animals. In so doing, he founded the sciences of biology and zoology. Meanwhile, his friend, Theophrastus, closely examined thousands of plant species. Many of his conclusions were both brilliant and correct. In his honor, modern scientists call him the father of botany.

Other Greeks continued to search for the *physis,* a substance thought to be the basis of all matter. Early thinkers had been unable to find it. But in the 400s BC Democritus and Leucippus succeeded. They proposed that all matter is made up of incredibly tiny particles. They called them "atoms." The world's first atomic theory was mostly correct.

Still other Greek thinkers made important medical advances. One of those thinkers was Hippocrates. In the late 400s BC he and his students wrote many books. They described the human body and its diseases. They also argued that doctors have a duty to help people. One of those writings contains a doctor's oath. It states that a physician should never harm anyone. Modern doctors swear to a version of this so-called Hippocratic Oath. For these contributions to medicine, Hippocrates is today recognized as the father of modern medicine.

SPLITTING IT ALL UP: THE BOUNDARIES OF KNOWLEDGE

Today, almost all scientists specialize in one branch of science. So an astronomer deals only with studying the stars, planets, and other heavenly bodies. But the early Greek scientists were also philosophers. Thus, while describing atoms, Democritus wrote about the soul and the nature of goodness. During his lifetime, however, something crucial happened. Namely, science and philosophy began to separate. That event shaped the way modern scientists and philosophers see and define the world. The driving force behind this trend was one of history's most influential thinkers. His name was Socrates. An Athenian, he was short and shabby-looking. Some people viewed him as a sort of hobo.

FACT

Socrates wanted people to find both life's and their own truths. To do that he needed a way to examine them. So he invented one. He asked them a series of questions. Little by little the answers led to the truth. Philosophers still sometimes use that approach—the Socratic method—today.

Yet several well-to-do and influential citizens held him in high regard. Among them was the young Plato.

Socrates spent most of his days wandering through the city's streets. Often he stopped people at random. He urged them to examine their lives. He asked, did they always act in ethical ways? Were they good? Honest? Just? In this way, he pushed them to search for life's truths and realities. Earlier Greek thinkers had examined these concepts. But Socrates devoted all his time to philosophy.

Over time, other thinkers explored these same weighty concepts. Plato devoted much of his time to philosophy. So did Aristotle and other later Greeks and Romans. In early modern times, philosophy was taught in universities across Europe. Today, nearly every college offers philosophy courses. Perhaps you'll take a philosophy course one day!

Meanwhile, science is equally ingrained in modern society. When Europe rediscovered its Greek roots, modern thinkers like Copernicus took note. They were inspired to carry on the studies of nature the Greeks had begun. Today, scientists in numerous fields continue to expand the boundaries of knowledge. Their inventions make people's lives easier and more comfortable. The Greek philosopher-scientists could never have predicted this. They could not imagine the fantastic forces they had set in motion. Those forces have already made billions of lives longer and more fulfilling. And there is no end in sight.

Archimedes was perhaps the greatest mathematician of ancient times. It was said that he invented giant weapons to fight the Romans.

THE MATH WHIZ OF SYRACUSE

Among the many different kinds of ancient Greek scientists, some were mathematicians. The greatest Greek math whiz of all was Archimedes. He was born in 287 BC in Syracuse. It was the largest Greek city-state on the island of Sicily. As a young man he visited Alexandria, Egypt, where he also probably studied. Returning to Syracuse, he made several important discoveries. One was that every substance has a specific density, or compactness. This became known as "Archimedes' principle." He also calculated the mathematical relationship between the volumes of cylinders and spheres. In addition, Archimedes was a brilliant inventor. He experimented with various sizes of levers. Some ancient writers claim he built a complex system of levers and pulleys. With it he moved a large merchant ship using muscle power alone. Other accounts report he constructed giant catapults. With these he tried to repel a Roman assault on Syracuse. But the attackers took the city and Archimedes was killed during the fighting.

CHAPTER 2

WE RULE! PEOPLE'S RIGHT TO GOVERN THEMSELVES

According to the Pew Research Center, which collects facts and stats, more than half the world's nations are democracies. In those countries, the people elect their leaders. That way each citizen has a say in government. Also, each citizen is equal in the eyes of the law. They have freedom of speech. People can worship as they like. Americans take pride in their democracy. So do people in Canada, Great Britain, and France. They are built around a key democratic concept. Namely, a government should be run *by* the people and *for* the people.

WHEN ARISTOCRATS RULED

The United States, which formed in 1776, was the first modern democracy. But there were democracies in ancient times, too, thanks to the Greeks. In fact, democracy may well be the current world's greatest gift from ancient Greece. The democratic concept was born there sometime in the 700s BC. This was when city-states were emerging in Greece. At first many of these communities were run by local chieftains. As time went on, however, town councils replaced them. Such a council was made up of a small group of local men. (Women were considered second-class citizens. They were not allowed to partake in politics.)

Each councilor was an aristocrat. That term comes from the Greek word *aristos*, meaning "best." The councilmen saw themselves as the fittest men to rule. This is because they were from the community's richest land-owning families. Often one or more local aristocrats ran the community on a daily basis. These managers were called "archons." There was also an assembly, or meeting, of the local soldiers. They were mainly farmers who doubled as fighters when outsiders threatened the community. By tradition, the soldiers voiced their approval of the aristocrats' decisions. Beyond that, the Assembly had no power or clout.

MOVING TOWARD DEMOCRACY

In the U.S. and other modern democracies, when people are unhappy with their leaders they can and do stage protests. That is what happened in ancient

Athens. Before the late 600s BC, the citizens of most Greek city-states were powerless to defy their councils and archons. Athenians proved to be an exception, however. The local farmers and other common people decided they wanted more say in government. So they started to challenge the aristocrats' authority. This led to outbreaks of fighting. Some aristocrats and their supporters were killed.

The hostility between commoners and aristocrats continued to worsen until 594 BC. That year Athens was on the verge of full-scale civil war. At the last minute, however, the leaders of the two sides struck a deal. To avoid disaster, they appealed to a citizen named Solon. Athenians of all walks of life viewed him as wise and fair. So they asked him to reform the government. Everyone agreed to accept whatever changes he made.

Solon first overhauled the laws. He made them fairer to both aristocrats and commoners. Next he created a new social system that made it possible for commoners to become archons. Also, the members of the old soldiers' Assembly gained more authority. They now voted to elect the archons. In addition, Solon introduced the Council. It was a group of 400 men chosen by lot, or random drawing. Meeting regularly, they decided which community projects needed approval. The archons then made sure those tasks were done.

THE ASSEMBLY'S SWEEPING DEMOCRATIC POWERS

All U.S. citizens are free to attend and speak out at meetings of their local town councils. That reminds them that they have a real say in how they are governed. Similarly, Solon's reforms gave the Athenian commoners some say in how they were ruled. That made Athens partially democratic. Full-blown democracy emerged a little less than a century later. In 508 BC Cleisthenes, another reformer, came on the scene. He and his supporters transformed Athens' government in dramatic ways.

The biggest single change was a major expansion of the Assembly's authority. All adult male citizens could attend its meetings. (Women and enslaved men were excluded.) The meetings took place on a rocky hill, called the Pnyx, not far from the Acropolis. Usually between 4,000 and 6,000 men attended. If attendance was less, government officials worried that the democratic

Cleisthenes was an Athenian nobleman who sought the support of the common people. In return for that support, he majorly expanded the city-state's democracy.

system might weaken. One attempt to remedy this developed for times when too few citizens showed up for an assembly meeting. Some specially trained enslaved workers carrying ropes dipped in red paint ran through the streets. When they found a man playing hooky, they swatted him. Anyone with telltale red marks on his clothes had to pay a fine.

The Assembly now had truly sweeping powers. Its members debated and voted on all issues affecting the community. They could make new laws or get rid of old ones. They could also grant citizenship or strip someone of it. In addition, the Assembly approved funds for building projects. It declared war and made peace.

It founded colonies and much more. No other democratic body in history has ever had so much authority over a nation or people.

The Pnyx Hill is located not far from Athens's more famous hill, the Acropolis. Meetings of the Assembly took place atop the Pnyx.

MEETINGS OF THE ATHENS ASSEMBLY

The Assembly lay at the core of Athens' democracy. That citizen body met about every ten days. The meetings took place outside on the Pnyx. It was a hill located a few hundred yards from the Acropolis. Each meeting started with a prayer. Most often it was directed at the city's divine protector, Athena. (All Greeks saw her as the goddess of war and wisdom.) There might also be a sacrifice. It consisted of killing a pig or other animal to appease the gods. Then, one by one, citizens stood on a platform and addressed the crowd. Its members listened intently. They shouted their approval to some speakers. Others got booed. After discussing an issue, the citizens voted on it. The majority always won. Modern historians have closely studied the Athenian Assembly.

In ancient Athens, the job of a Council member was to prepare the list of topics for the Assembly to discuss. Councilors also came up with ideas for new laws. These went to the Assembly to be voted for or against. Today the U.S. government's legislative branch, the Senate and the House of Representatives, have committees which perform in a similar way to the Council. These committees prepare findings to present to the Senate or House for a vote.

In Cleisthenes' reform, the Council expanded from 400 to 500 members. Each member served for a year. He could serve a second year, if chosen. But he could not serve a third until later in life. That ensured a few eager individuals would not wield power for too long. Also, it gave every man a chance to serve at least once in his lifetime.

Meanwhile, other citizens took part in the justice system. Each year 6,000 men were chosen by lot to serve on juries. A typical jury had several hundred members. This made tampering with a trial impossible.

FACT

Athenian democracy featured a way to get rid of corrupt or unpopular leaders. It was called "ostracism." Each male citizen found a piece of broken pottery. On it he wrote the name of the leader he desired to remove. A leader who received 6,000 of these negative votes was banished for ten years.

No one could afford to bribe or dared to threaten so many people. There were no professional prosecutors or defense attorneys. The accuser and accused in a case gathered their own evidence and witnesses. They then presented them to the jury. In modern democracies prosecutors and defense attorneys do these jobs. Otherwise, today's juries operate similarly to those in ancient Athens.

REPRESENTATIVE VS. DIRECT DEMOCRACY

Athens' democracy was soon copied by other Greeks. By the 300s BC, most Greek city-states had adopted some form of democracy. But these democracies did not last long. In the centuries that followed, Rome conquered the Greek lands. The Greeks were eventually ruled by Roman emperors. Later still, Greco-Roman civilization declined and vanished.

Many centuries passed. The idea of people directly governing themselves remained a distant memory. Finally, however, the U.S. founders revived it. They and the leaders of other modern democracies altered some aspects of the older Greek version. The biggest change was based on the enormous size of modern nations. The population of a Greek city-state numbered in the thousands. So most citizens could stand on a hillside together and vote. That made democracy very direct. By contrast, most modern nations have millions of citizens. No hillside or building

In the city of Athens, magnificent ruins rest atop the Acropolis as a remnant of its former greatness. The ruins are dominated by the Parthenon.

can contain them all. So people in each local area elect someone to represent them. Those representatives meet, debate, and vote in an assembly-like congress.

Today the U.S. president has numerous duties. The president oversees the government on a daily basis. The president also signs new laws and meets with foreign diplomats. In contrast, the Athenian democracy had no president. This was because the Assembly itself did most of what modern presidents do. Despite these and other differences, modern democracies were strongly inspired by Greek models. They utilize the same noble principles born long ago in Greece. Chief among them is the right of any nation's citizens to rule themselves.

CHAPTER 3

SHAPING UP! GREAT ARCHITECTURE FOR THE AGES

Have you ever visited the U.S. Supreme Court building in Washington, D.C.? If you haven't you're in for a real treat. Ever since it was completed in 1935 it has been viewed as one of the world's most majestic structures. Its front porch is particularly impressive. A grand stone stairway leads to a row of eight tall, massive marble columns. These support a triangular gable—the pointed section just beneath the roof.

Even if you haven't seen the Supreme Court building in person, odds are you are very familiar with its style. The image of a row of columns topped by a decorated gable has come to be seen as noble-looking. For that reason, it has been used in thousands of other modern structures. Besides courthouses, they include other government buildings and banks.

HOUSES FOR THE GODS

Although the columns-and-gable style is widely used today, keep in mind that it is far from new. The truth is that modern architects borrowed it from the ancient Greeks. It is often called "Greek temple architecture." This is because the Greeks invented it for their religious temples. They also used it in other public buildings.

Another crucial point is that Greek temples were not used the same way religious buildings are today. People gather inside modern churches or mosques to worship. In contrast, no public worship took place inside Greek temples. Instead, those structures were meant to be houses for the gods. All Greeks recognized and revered the same gods. Yet each city-state had its favorite. That so-called divine patron was thought to protect the city and its residents. Moreover, people believed the patron deity sometimes visited the community. And while there he or she needed a place to reside. Temples served that purpose. Guarding the local god's privacy was seen as super-important. So the altars used in public worship were outside. Often they stood on the front steps.

The Greeks began erecting these houses for the gods sometime before the 700s BC. The first examples were small and used fragile materials. The walls were made of wood or sun-dried mud-bricks or both. Roofs were made of thatch (bundled plant stems). Those materials decay quickly. So all of the earliest Greek temples disappeared long ago. Luckily, a handful of little pottery models of them have survived. They show a rectangular structure. They had a front porch featuring a triangular gable beneath a slanted roof. Architects call such a gable a "pediment." Supporting the pediment were two to four thin wooden columns.

As time went on, these early temples rapidly grew in size. They also became more complex. The number of columns increased, for instance. Soon each temple had rows of them on all four sides. A back porch was also added. Each porch came to have a broad staircase in front. In addition, colorful decorations appeared in the pediments and above the columns.

HIGH STANDARDS

If you ever visit Baltimore, Maryland, try to visit the Baltimore Basilica. It's a Catholic church and is actually one of the most beautiful American structures purposely built to resemble a Greek temple. The towering front columns are made of marble. In comparison, the earliest Greek columns were made of wood. But a major turning point occurred in the mid-600s BC. To make the thatch roofs last longer, builders started using more durable pottery roofing tiles. But these were much heavier than thatch. The wooden columns and walls couldn't bear the load. So the builders switched to stone. All-stone temples were soon standard. The ruins of these structures can still be seen in Greece.

One of the world's best-preserved ancient Greek temples is the temple of Hera at Paestum. Paestum was originally the Greek city of Poseidonia that once prospered in southern Italy.

The most prominent Ionic-style Greek temple was dedicated to Artemis, goddess of wild animals. The structure was erected at Ephesus, in what is now western Turkey. It was by far the biggest temple in the Greek lands. Its length stretched 425 feet (130 meters). This is even larger than a modern football field.

An artist's conception depicts the gigantic temple of Artemis, at Ephesus. It was so impressive that it made the list of the Seven Wonders of the Ancient World.

The architects and builders also strove for quality. They tried to erect temples that were well-proportioned and beautiful. For decades they searched for just the right balance. By the mid-500s BC they found it. They agreed that the most pleasing ratio of length to width was two-to-one. Thereafter, nearly all temples had six columns on each end and thirteen on each side.

TEMPLES FOR ZEUS, APOLLO, AND ATHENA

Today, when people climb the well-worn stone stairs on the western side of Athens' Acropolis, a magical sight greets them. It consists of the regal ruins of the Parthenon. That stately temple honored Athena, goddess of war and wisdom. When new, it was one of the many temples the Greeks erected from the late 500s BC on.

Some were both splendid and widely renowned. One was at Olympia, in southwestern Greece. It was the site of the famous Olympic Games. The temple, built between 470 and 457 BC, was dedicated to the king of the Greek gods, Zeus. Inside it a giant statue of Zeus sat on a magnificent throne. No less celebrated by the Greeks was Apollo's temple at Delphi, in central Greece. It was completed around 370 BC. Apollo was the god of prophecy, or seeing into the future. The temple received numerous visitors, many of whom hoped to glimpse their own futures. They questioned its priestess, known as the Delphic oracle. It was thought that her answers came from Apollo himself.

These temples were among the finest the Greeks ever built. Yet they never achieved the fame that Athens' Parthenon did. Modern architects often call the Parthenon the most perfect structure ever created. The Athenians had earlier erected other temples for Athena, mostly atop the Acropolis. But they were destroyed when invaders briefly occupied the city in 480 BC.

Some Athenians wanted to replace those structures. Pericles, a major champion of democracy, was one of them. He became a driving force behind a new and immense construction project. Beginning in the 440s BC, it totally transformed the Acropolis. Thousands of workers labored for years to create new temples, shrines, and other buildings.

The Parthenon was the crown jewel of the new temple complex. It was conceived on a grander scale than the Temple of Zeus at Olympia. Instead of six columns in the front, the Parthenon had eight. And rather than thirteen columns on each side, it had seventeen. Also, it was covered by superb sculptures of people and animals. And inside stood a towering statue of Athena adorned in battle armor. The U.S. Supreme Court building may not have such an impressive statue, but its architecture echoes the noble balance of the Parthenon.

LIKE MINIATURE TEMPLES

The Greeks used their temple architectural style for more than just temples. They applied it in some smaller structures as well. One was called a "treasury." City-states erected treasuries to store gold and other valuables. Several, including Athens, built them at Delphi. They lined a winding path near Apollo's temple, home of the famous Delphic oracle. Those treasuries held the gifts that religious pilgrims from far and wide presented Apollo. Another structure that looked like a tiny temple was the fountain house. Each was built beside a stream. Water flowed from the stream into a holding tank in the building. People who lived nearby turned a faucet on an outer wall. They filled their buckets. Then they carried the water home.

THE RAVAGES OF TIME

When tourists from around the globe visit the Parthenon and other Greek temples today, they see only broken fragments of their past splendor. This is because wars, earthquakes, floods, and the ravages of time all took their toll. In the Parthenon's case, it remained mostly intact until 1687. That year foreign attackers fired cannons at the Acropolis. Containers of gunpowder stored in the aged temple exploded, and the damage was severe.

Even in its ruined state, however, the Parthenon was still noble-looking. So it thrilled foreigners who visited Athens. Among them were German, English, and U.S. architects. They began to copy its form in new buildings. William Strickland designed the first major American structure to use Greek temple architecture. It was Philadelphia's Second Bank of the United States, completed in 1824. By the close of that century, thousands of other examples existed around the globe. The Greeks' vision of great architecture had triumphed, both in their own age and for all ages.

FACT

The statue of Athena that stood inside the Parthenon was designed by Phidias. Modern historians often call him the ancient world's greatest sculptor. The statue was almost 40 feet (12 m) tall. It was made of wood, ivory, and about 2,500 pounds (1,134 kilograms) of pure gold.

Two views of the Parthenon show what it looked like when newly built and how it appears today. The cutaway in the drawing (top) reveals Phidias's huge statue of Athena inside.

CHAPTER 4

GOOD SPORTS: ORIGINS OF THE OLYMPIC GAMES

Every four years, athletes from more than 200 nations come together in different cities for a huge event—the Olympic Games. The world's greatest athletes compete in dozens of popular sports. Among them are track and field's running, jumping, and throwing events and swimming and diving. Others include wrestling, boxing, cycling, soccer, and basketball. More than 3 billion people worldwide watch the games on TV. That is nearly half of the global population! Even bigger audiences are expected for future Olympic games.

A STRONG LOVE OF SPORTS

The first modern Olympics occurred in Athens, Greece, in 1896. That city was chosen to honor the games' ancient Greek origins. The earliest versions took place in the 700s and 600s BC. This was when city-states were emerging all over Greece. These tiny, fiercely independent nations frequently fought among themselves. Now and then, however, they came together in peace. Their athletes met at Olympia, in southwestern Greece.

Along with the Greek language and worship of the same gods, the love of sports was one of the three main cultural factors that all Greeks shared. No one knows exactly when this strong love of sports began. It appears to have been part of the Greeks' cultural DNA, so to speak. What is certain is that in each city-state men of all ages regularly exercised together. (Women were excluded.

The opening ceremonies of the first Olympic Games held in modern times were attended by more than 60,000 people. The 1896 games introduced the first marathon race.

It was thought to be improper for females to socially mix with men outside the family.)

Each city-state had at least one gym. They started as open gathering places. From there, they evolved into something much closer to the gyms we know today. They were areas for training complete with baths and dressing rooms. And the larger city-states, like Athens, had several gyms. Not every Greek male was muscular and athletic, as modern movies often depict. But all men strove for what they saw as the ideal. It was a sound mind in a strong body.

The gyms were more than just places to work out. They also held informal athletic contests. These included wrestling matches, footraces, and discus and javelin throwing. Contests were popular all over Greece. At some point men from one city began challenging the men from neighboring cities. Before long, every city-state took part. This marked the birth of Panhellenic, or "all-Greek," athletic games. These major competitions were not only about sports. They were also religious festivals designed to honor the gods.

Over the centuries four major Panhellenic games came to be held. One—the Nemean Games—was held every two years and honored Zeus. The Isthmian Games was also held every two years. It was dedicated to Poseidon, god of the seas. There was also the Pythian Games, honoring Apollo. It took place at Delphi every four years.

THE TRUCE AND TRIP TO OLYMPIA

Modern Olympic athletes train extremely hard in their various events. In fact, many years of training are typically needed to prepare for a competition held only once every four years. The same was true in ancient Greece. There the most prominent of the four major athletic competitions—the Olympics—took place every four years. Devoted to Zeus, it was held at Olympia. That place was not a city. The city-state of Elis held authority over the sacred site. So the Eleans had the honor of hosting the games. As hosts of the games, every four years the Eleans sent out three heralds known as the "Truce-Bearers." Their job was to go to every Greek state and announce the exact date of the upcoming games.

The heralds also declared the Olympic truce. During this three-month period all Greeks were expected to refrain from fighting. This ensured that athletes and

spectators could safely travel to and from Olympia. Any city that violated the truce had to pay a huge fine.

Reaching Olympia, the travelers made their way to the athletic sites. One was a hippodrome. It was a long, oval-shaped outdoor track for horse and chariot races. There was also a wrestling arena and a stadium for track and field events.

THE OLYMPIC PROGRAM

Today, the summer Olympics lasts just over two weeks. In contrast, the original Greek version lasted five days. On the first day, several religious ceremonies took place. Addressing Zeus, the athletes swore they would

FACT

The 26-mile-long marathon footrace is a regular event in the modern Olympics. But it was not part of the ancient Olympics. A modern entry in the Olympics, it honors a legendary long run made by an Athenian soldier. Supposedly he brought his countrymen news of their army's victory over foreign invaders.

compete honestly. The judges also took an oath. They promised to be fair and never take bribes. After the oaths, people prayed and presented offerings to Zeus.

The athletic events began on the second day. Most athletes competed in the nude. This was partly to honor the gods. The belief was that the gods gave humans their own divine, and therefore ideal, physical form. In the morning, the horse and chariot races took place in the hippodrome. That afternoon the spectators watched the popular pentathlon. It consisted of five events: sprinting, the long jump, the discus toss, the javelin throw, and wrestling. Later, in the evening, they enjoyed a lavish feast.

Day three at Olympia witnessed more religious ceremonies. In one, the athletes and Elean officials sacrificed a hundred oxen to appease Zeus. Then came several events for boys younger than eighteen. During the fourth day, the adult athletes competed in the main footraces. The combat events also occurred that day. Wrestling and boxing were among them.

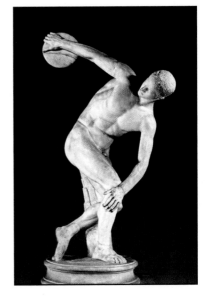

The statue of a discus thrower by the Greek sculptor Myron is one of the most famous of all ancient artworks. The discus throw is still a popular event in modern track meets everywhere.

There was also the *pankration,* a very rough combination of wrestling and boxing. Some of those who did it were seriously injured and a few died.

On the Olympics' fifth and final day, more religious rituals and feasts were held. The highlight, however, was the ceremony for the victorious athletes. Each received a crown of wild olive branches. These had no monetary value, but they enormously improved the victors' reputations. Winning an event at Olympia was like winning the Super Bowl today. Also, the winners received valuable rewards when they returned home. Some got cash prizes. Others received free meals for life.

CELEBRATING HUMANITY

Even after Rome conquered the Greek lands, the games remained widely popular. One Roman emperor— Nero—actually competed in them. This changed after Rome became Christian, however. Christian emperors banned worship of the old Greco-Roman gods. They shut down the Olympics in the 390s.

Many centuries passed. Around the 1600s, some well-to-do Englishmen tried to stage athletic events similar to the Olympics. A similar attempt occurred in France in the 1700s. Others happened in Sweden and Greece in the early 1800s. But none of these efforts gained wide popularity.

Success came later, in 1894, Frenchmen Pierre de Coubertin established the International Olympic Committee (IOC). Two years later the IOC staged the first modern Olympics in Athens. Fourteen nations sent a total of 241 athletes. It was a small beginning. But it rapidly grew. Later, the IOC added the winter version of the Olympics. It holds contests in ice-skating, skiing, and other winter sports. Another expansion was the Paralympics. It features events for disabled athletes. Without realizing it, the Greeks had instilled their deep love of sports in future generations. What began long ago as an event for Greeks only has become a celebration for all of humanity.

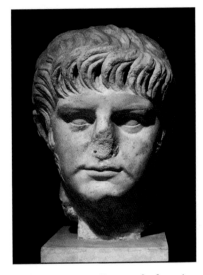

The Roman emperor Nero was far from the great athlete he thought he was. But Rome then ruled the Greeks. So they could not stop him from competing in the Olympics.

FACT

The ancient Olympic event called the *pankration* is not part of today's Olympics. But a modern version of it is widely popular. Many of the moves in professional mixed martial arts (MMA) closely resemble those of the *pankration*.

THE WOMEN'S GAMES

Greek women were not allowed to watch or directly compete at Olympia. Much later—in the first century BC—women received permission to watch the Pythian, Isthmian, and Nemean games. They were still barred from the all-male Olympics, however. But by that time women already competed at Olympia. Possibly as early as 500 BC, women were allowed to have a separate competition there. It was called the Heraea. That name reflected that it honored Zeus's wife, Hera. The Heraea was held every four years. But it occurred in a different month than the men's games. Sixteen Elean women organized the festival. The female athletes took part in a single event. It was a footrace a bit less than two football fields in length. There were numerous heats and semi-finals, though. So, many women got to compete. The winners received crowns made of olive-branches. They also shared slabs of meat from a cow the Eleans sacrificed to Hera.

CHAPTER 5

UPSTAGED: BIRTH OF THE DRAMATIC ARTS

The *Avengers* films have been immensely popular worldwide. So have TV series such as *Once Upon a Time* and the Broadway musical *Hamilton*. Aside from their fame, they all have something else in common. They owe their existence to the ancient Greeks.

Theater and drama were born in Athens some twenty-five centuries ago. Actors, plays, costumes, and even acting awards all originated there. After that, for many centuries audiences gathered in theaters to watch actors perform. Much later, in the twentieth century, the technology developed to transfer those performances to film.

TELLING A GOD'S LIFE STORY

People attend plays or go to the movies because they're looking to be entertained. They want the actors, words, music, and special effects to take them to another place or another time or both. What is little known is that these fun pastimes actually *came* from a very different place and time. The theater evolved from ancient Greek religious rituals. At first they were connected to Dionysus, the Greek god of fertility—the richness of the soil. In particular he oversaw vineyards and their chief product, wine. Greeks everywhere saw him as a fun-loving deity. Artists often depicted him as a bit tipsy from drinking too much wine. However, sometimes he also displayed a serious side. Humans who angered him could suffer harsh punishment. The myths about him featured both his playful and vengeful sides.

Together, those myths told the story of Dionysus's life. At least as far back as the 700s BC, the Greeks appeased and honored him by frequently retelling that story. They did it in a special ceremony. Dozens or more of the faithful gathered together. A few stood before the others and sang sacred songs. The words recalled the god's various exploits. These verses became

An ancient statue of Dionysus portrays his role as the deity of vineyards and wine. The solemn ceremonies in which people worshiped him grew into the first theatrical shows.

known as dithyramb. In time, the singers also danced to the music. Later still, they added some special gestures and costumes to enliven the storytelling. Overall, their presentation became a kind of performance. The other worshippers who watched them were, in a sense, their audience.

As time passed, the dithyramb became even more elaborate. It appears that it developed the fastest in Athens. There, the rituals began telling other gods' stories too. Also, by the early 500s BC these ceremonies included myths about popular human heroes.

THESPIS'S WINNING IDEA

What is your favorite new TV show? Odds are you like it because it seems fresh and exciting. The people of Athens thought the same in 534 BC during an annual religious festival honoring Dionysus. As in other festivals, there were prayers and offerings to the god. But this version also introduced a new feature—a contest. In it men competed to see who could compose the best new versions of the dithyramb.

A participant named Thespis was the victor. His winning idea was to go beyond merely telling about Dionysus and other characters. He actually pretended to *be* one of those characters. That is, he *took on the role* of Dionysus or someone else. In so doing, he stood apart from the singers and dancers. While in character, he exchanged verses with them. Though still simple and small-scale, it was the world's first play. Also, he was the first known actor. In this way the theater was born. In Thespis's honor, people today sometimes refer to actors as "thespians."

This new approach to storytelling was an instant hit. Many Athenians wanted to either take part or watch. In response, Thespis and others like him continued to experiment. They added more and more elements of real life. Gods and superhuman heroes were no longer the only characters. People, from kings to messengers, were now included. Another novel idea was to have a single actor play multiple characters. The audience had to be able to tell one character from another, so someone suggested using masks. When the actor donned a "god" mask, he became a god. Similarly, he might put on a "king" mask, a "soldier" mask, or some other mask. All such actors were men. It was seen as improper for women to perform in public.

FINANCING PLAY PRODUCTION

Do you enjoy TV shows and movies about superheroes? Or are you more into murder mysteries, or maybe comedies? Whatever your taste in entertainment might be, you aren't alone. Hundreds of millions of people worldwide enjoy such shows. Similarly, after the Athenians invented the theater, that new dramatic art form rapidly expanded. Moreover, local residents were not the only spectators. People from other city-states often attended the plays. This greatly enhanced Athens' reputation and influence. Along with superb art and architecture, the theater made the city Greece's leading cultural center.

Athenian leaders naturally wanted to retain that important status. So the government financially supported play production. It paid the actors, for example. It also built and maintained a structure in which to present the plays. The world's first theater became known as the Theater of Dionysus. It was located near the base of the Acropolis. There was a semicircular outdoor stage—the orchestra. Facing it was a semicircular seating section built into the hill's rising slope.

At its largest expansion, the Theater of Dionysus sat about 17,000 people. What are considered some of the greatest plays ever written were first presented there.

Meanwhile, money was needed for other aspects of play production. The funds came from a few wealthy citizens. They paid for costumes, sets, musicians, and so forth. These backers were called *choregoi*.

TRAGEDY AND COMEDY

One of the most famous and widely watched TV specials are the annual Academy Awards. Also called the Oscars, they honor the best film actors, writers, and directors. Would you be surprised to learn that such awards are not new and that the Greeks came up with them too? The truth is that the fifth century, or 400s BC proved to be Athens' golden age of theater and drama.

FACT

The ancient theater at Epidaurus, in southern Greece, features superior sound production. An actor on the stage can be heard clearly in the back row—200 feet (61 m) away. Modern experts think the shape of the stone seats causes this amazing effect.

Dozens of playwrights competed. The most talented had their plays presented in Dionysus's festival. From those, a panel of ten judges selected the best. They also chose the best actors, and all the winners received awards. The Oscars are simply the modern version of those ancient prizes!

Most of these plays that competed for awards disappeared long ago. But a few by the four finest playwrights of the era did survive. Three of those dramatists penned tragedies. Each tragic play examined some of life's sadder, unhappier aspects. Aeschylus was the earliest of the three great tragic playwrights. He wrote as many as eighty-two plays. Of those, seven survive complete. It was said that he won the best play award thirteen times. He also introduced a second main actor. Like the first actor, he wore various masks. That doubled the number of characters a play could depict.

The other two leading tragic playwrights were Sophocles and Euripides. Sophocles utilized a third and maybe a fourth actor. That further expanded drama's storytelling potential. He wrote around 123 plays. Seven of those plays have survived. The most famous is *Oedipus the King* (ca. 429 BC). Many modern drama critics call it the greatest tragedy ever written. Euripides wrote about 92 plays. Nineteen of them still exist. They frequently feature strong female characters. Perhaps the most famous example is *Medea* (431 BC). The title character's husband is unfaithful to her. To punish him, she kills their children.

The fourth great fifth-century BC playwright was Aristophanes. He wrote comedies. Of his forty-four plays, eleven have survived. The comic plays of that era were usually very frank and daring. Often they poked fun at leaders and other prominent people. They also used vulgar jokes and slapstick humor.

THE FIRST "SPECIAL EFFECTS"

Today, big-budget movies are filled with awesome special effects. The earliest versions of them appeared in ancient Greek plays. These were crude by today's standards. But at the time they amazed and excited audiences. One was called a "tableau machine." It was a platform that moved on small wheels. Murders occurred offstage. Right after such a killing, someone pushed the machine onto the stage. On it were the murderer and victim, spattered with blood. The actors were frozen in a snapshot-like pose. The audience members gasped and booed the murderer. Even more dramatic was the so-called "god from the machine." In the exciting climax of many plays, a god often appeared. Commonly he or she did something that ended the play on a positive note. The actor playing that deity wore a harness. It was attached to a crane that swung him high above the stage. The audience welcomed the god with applause and cheers.

THE FOREMOST FORM OF ENTERTAINMENT

By the dawn of the twentieth century, London, New York, and other major cities had thriving theater districts. Then came the invention of film. It enormously expanded the dramatic arts' impact. These events would not have occurred if it was not for the huge popularity of ancient Athenian drama. Over time other Greek city-states erected theaters and presented plays too. Moreover, the Romans adopted the art form, giving it their own spin. They too turned out both tragedies and comedies.

It is true that most of that ancient play production stopped when Rome declined in the fifth century AD. However, this lapse proved only temporary. In the 1400s and 1500s, Europeans rediscovered their Greco-Roman cultural heritage. Ancient playwrights' works began to be performed again. The French and other Europeans wrote new plays as well. They also built new theaters to perform them in. The same thing happened in America and other places Europeans had colonized. Today, storytelling using actors is by far the world's foremost form of entertainment. For that, people everywhere owe the ancient Greeks a debt too big to measure or repay.

FACT

Sophocles' great play *Oedipus the King*, is about a man who never knew his birth parents. As an adult, he becomes king of the city of Thebes. In time he learns that a man he killed years before was his father. Moreover, his present wife is actually his mother. Horrified, Oedipus rips out his own eyes.

CHAPTER 6

IT'S LEGENDARY: GREEK MYTHOLOGY'S TIMELESS TALES

Today's entertainment media are filled with popular fictional characters. Myths are a major source of those characters. Those ancient tales come from a wide range of cultures. The mighty Thor came from the Norse myths, for instance. And British mythology produced King Arthur and his knights of the round table.

However, by far the most numerous legendary characters come from the Greek myths. They pervade all aspects of modern culture. Hercules is only one example. (The Greeks called him Heracles. Today he is better known by his Roman name, Hercules.) His father was a god and his mother a mortal woman. The divine spark in him made him incredibly strong. In fact, he was the strongest man in the world and a true hero.

He has appeared in dozens of modern movies, TV shows, and video games. His stories and those of other Greek myths remain alive in the public imagination. Endlessly retold, they continue to pass from one generation to the next.

STAYING ON THE GODS' GOOD SIDE

The muscular Greek hero Heracles, whom the Romans called Hercules, is almost always depicted bearded. Myths claim he wore the skin of a lion that he killed with his bare hands.

If your parents tell you not to do something but you do it anyway, you might be punished. The ancient Greeks had a similar relationship with the gods who appeared in their myths. In fact, those stories were closely connected to religion. Most of those tales featured one or more gods. And even the ones about human heroes usually involved the gods in some way. Moreover, worship of the gods was central to Greek life at least from the 700s BC on. Nearly all Greeks were very pious. They observed numerous religious rituals and prayed often.

The myths the Greeks cherished explained how the gods came to be. They also told those deities' life stories. In addition, they described the gods' appearance and their relationship with humans. From those tales the Greeks learned that the gods looked exactly like people. They displayed human emotions as well. Also like people, they sometimes made mistakes. The myths describe the gods losing their tempers, fighting among themselves, and having love affairs and children.

The gods were far from perfect. Yet the Greeks felt those beings must be respected. One reason was that the gods were immortal. Also, they possessed enormous power. That power, the myths showed, could either help or destroy humanity. Through regular worship, therefore, people could please the gods and stay on their good side.

THE AGE OF HEROES

Today, Americans enjoy and pass on all sorts of tall tales. One describes George Washington chopping down a cherry tree. Another claims there was a friendly giant logger named Paul Bunyan in the northern midwest. Similarly, the classical Greeks told and retold their many myths. They believed that those stories described real events. For example, people accepted that the gods had arisen from Chaos. At first the cosmos was a swirling mass of jumbled matter, one myth said. Some elements within that mass were alive. They mated, giving rise to powerful beings. In turn, those beings had children—the first race of gods. They were known as the Titans.

A drawing shows a portion of the sculptures decorating the Great Altar at Pergamon, a Greek city in what is now Turkey. It depicts Zeus battling with several members of a race of giants.

Other myths told about the leading Titan, Kronos. Afraid his children would someday turn on him, he swallowed each when it was born. One baby, Zeus, escaped, however. He was raised in secret and when grown came back and overthrew Kronos. Zeus and his siblings and children became the second divine race—the Olympians.

The Olympians proceeded to create humans, or mortals. Some mortals interacted with the gods. Of those humans, a few were fearless heroes, like Hercules. They rid the world of hideous monsters and evil tyrants. All these things happened in the dim past, the Greeks believed. They called that long-ago era the Age of Heroes.

For the Greeks, these and other myths seemed to explain all that humans needed to know about their world and past events. In reality, however, the past had been very different. The classical Greeks did not know that a prior high civilization had existed in their lands. Modern experts began digging up its remains on the Greek mainland around 1870 and in the Greek islands around 1900. That older civilization reached its height between about 1600 and 1200 BC. This was Greece's late Bronze Age. It roughly matches up with the Age of Heroes.

THE BRONZE AGE AND TROJAN WAR

Modern tourists regularly visit the ruins at Mycenae, in southern Greece. Especially popular is the Lion Gate. Its giant stones lead into a ruined, but still impressive, ancient fortress. Long ago that structure was the palace of the king of one of the small but powerful kingdoms the Bronze Age Greeks built. They had a workable writing system and various forms of art. Their civilization rapidly declined in the 1100s BC, however. Historians are still unsure why.

In the years that followed, the palaces were abandoned. Writing and most artistic skills disappeared. The survivors, most of them poor, lived in small villages. During this cultural dark age, people steadily lost their heritage. Memories of the earlier kingdoms grew faint

The Lion Gate at Mycenae was built during the late Bronze Age (about 1600 BC–1200 BC). Two carved lions face each other above the main entrance of the fortress.

and imprecise. Stories of past people and events morphed into colorful fables—the myths. Thus, some were loosely based on real past events. Other myths were likely simply made up.

In time, prosperity slowly returned to Greece. From the dark age emerged a new Greek civilization. Its people inherited the now extensive collection of myths. They especially enjoyed the stories of the Trojan War. Troy had been a wealthy city. It was located on the western coast of what is now Turkey. In the myths, a large Greek army sailed across the Aegean Sea. The force laid siege to Troy for ten years. During that period, some gods sided with the Trojans. Others backed the Greeks. Meanwhile, heroic warriors on both sides engaged in epic battles.

Greek writers told and retold these tales about the Trojan War. The most famous

A painting that shows soldiers fighting is from the so-called Ambrosian Iliad. Historians think that illustrated version of Homer's story of the Trojan War was created in the 300s.

version was the *Iliad*. It is credited to an early poet named Homer. The classical Greeks revered both him and the work. For centuries Greek schoolboys memorized and recited long sections of it. Homer's other great epic is the *Odyssey*. It traces the travels of the Greek king Odysseus. After helping to defeat Troy, he wandered the seas for ten years.

THE GREEK SPIRIT LIVES ON

Do you enjoy listening to people tell colorful stories? Perhaps you like telling them yourself. The ancient Romans certainly loved such tales, particularly the Greek myths. Several Romans wrote books that retold those stories. After Greco-Roman civilization declined, a few of those books survived. They introduced the Greek myths to the late medieval and early modern worlds. From the

The 2010 version of the *Clash of the Titans* starred Sam Worthington as Perseus and Liam Neeson as the god Zeus. In the movie, Perseus is trying to save his family in the middle of a war between gods.

PERSEUS AND MEDUSA

The *Clash of the Titans* movies and video game celebrate the Greek hero Perseus. He appears in one of the most famous of all myths. In the story, he wanted to slay the monstrous Medusa, who dwelled on a remote island. Her hair was a tangle of deadly snakes. But her scariest feature was her face. If a person or animal looked directly at her, he, she, or it quickly turned to stone. Hermes, the messenger god, gave Perseus sandals bearing little wings. This allowed the young man to fly to Medusa's island. Hermes also supplied a special cap. When Perseus put it on he became invisible. Thus, when he approached Medusa she could not see him. Another god had given Perseus a polished shield that acted as a mirror. With it the man gazed only on the monster's reflection. That kept him from turning to stone. Medusa had met her match. Perseus sliced off her head, ridding the world of her.

GLOSSARY

acropolis—in a Greek town, a central, fortified hill; the term in upper case (Acropolis) refers to the one in Athens

archon—a government administrator

aristocrat—a member of a group of people thought to be the best in some way, usually based on how much money they have; aristocrats are members of the highest social rank or nobility

choregoi—wealthy backers of plays and other cultural events

colony—a territory settled by people from another country and controlled by that country

cosmos—the universe as a complex system in harmony

deity—god or goddess

density—the amount of mass an object or substance has based on a unit of volume

dithyramb—sacred verses honoring the fertility god Dionysus

divine—holy; sacred

fertility—the richness of the soil

hippodrome—an outdoor racetrack for horse and chariot races

immortal—able to live forever

oracle—a priestess thought to be a medium between a god and humans

orchestra—in Greek theaters, the semicircular stone stage where the actors performed

ostracism—an Athenian custom in which the people voted to banish an unpopular leader

Panhellenic—open to Greeks from any and all Greek city-states

pankration—a very rough mixture of wrestling and boxing

pediment—the triangular gable on a Greek temple's front and back porches

philosopher—a person who studies ideas, the way people think, and the search for knowledge

philosophy—the study of truth, the nature of reality, and knowledge

physis—nature's first-principle, underlying physical basis

pious—someone who is pious practices his or her religion faithfully

prominent—widely and popularly known; leading

slapstick humor—comedy that stresses loud, rough action or horseplay

volume—the amount of space taken up by an object

vulgar—lacking in good manners or taste; crude

ADDITIONAL RESOURCES

Read More

Braun, Eric. *Greek Myths.* North Mankato, MN: Capstone Press, 2019.

Faust, Daniel R. *Ancient Greece.* New York: Gareth Stevens, 2019.

Randolph, Joanne, *Living and Working in Ancient Greece.* New York: Enslow Publishing, 2017.

Internet Sites

Ancient-Greece.org: The Parthenon
https://www.ancient-greece.org/architecture/parthenon.html

PBS: The Greeks: Crucible of Civilization
http://www.pbs.org/empires/thegreeks

Theoi Greek Mythology
http://www.theoi.com/

SELECT BIBLIOGRAPHY

Amemiya, Takeshi. *Economy and Economics of Ancient Greece*. London: Routledge, 2007.

Barnes, Jonathan, ed. *The Complete Works of Aristotle*, vols. 1 and 2. Princeton: Princeton University Press, 1984.

Barnes, Jonathan. *Early Greek Philosophy*. New York: Penguin, 2002.

Bertman, Stephen. *The Genesis of Science: The Story of Greek Imagination*. New York: Prometheus, 2010.

Bluemel, Carl. *Greek Sculptors at Work*. London: Phaidon, 1969.

Boardman, John. *Greek Sculpture: The Classical Period, a Handbook*. London: Thames & Hudson, 1991.

Burford, Alison. *Land and Labor in the Greek World*. Baltimore: The Johns Hopkins University Press, 2000.

Burkert, Walter. *Greek Religion: Archaic and Classical*. New York: Wiley-Blackwell, 2002.

Camp, John and Elizabeth Fisher. *The World of the Ancient Greeks*. London: Thames and Hudson, 2002.

Cartledge, Paul. *Ancient Greece: A Very Short Introduction*. New York: Oxford University Press, 2011.

Cartledge, Paul. *The Spartans: The World of the Warrior-Heroes of Ancient Greece, from Utopia to Crisis and Collapse*. New York: Overlook, 2003.

Casson, Lionel. *The Ancient Mariners*. Princeton: Princeton University Press, 1991.

Casson, Lionel. *Travel in the Ancient World*. Baltimore: Johns Hopkins University Press, 1994.

Chaline, Eric. *Ancient Greece as It Was: Exploring the City of Athens in 415. BC*. Guilford, CT: Lyons Press, 2011.

Couprie, Dirk L. *Heaven and Earth in Ancient Greek Cosmology: From Thales to Heraclides Ponticus*. New York: Springer, 2011.

Cuomo, S. *Technology and Culture in Greek and Roman Antiquity*. New York: Cambridge University Press, 2007.

De Camp, L. Sprague. *The Ancient Engineers*. New York: Ballantine, 1995.

De Souza, Philip. *The Greek and Persian Wars 499-386 BC*. London: Osprey, 2003.

Finley, M.I. *The Ancient Economy*. Berkeley: University of California Press, 1999.

Finley, M.I. and H.W. Pleket. *The Olympic Games: The First Thousand Years*. Mineola, NY: Dover, 2005.

Freeman, Charles. *Egypt, Greece, & Rome: Civilizations of the Ancient Mediterranean*. New York: Oxford University Press, 2014.

Freeman, Kathleen, *The Murder of Herodes and Other Trials from the Athenian Law Courts*. New York: W.W. Norton, 1963.

Garland, Robert. *Ancient Greece: Everyday Life in the Birthplace of Western Civilization*. New York: Sterling, 2013.

Golden, Mark. *Children and Childhood in Classical Athens*. Baltimore: Johns Hopkins University Press, 1990.

Grant, Michael and John Hazel. *Who's Who in Classical Mythology*. London: Routledge, 2002.

Grubbs, Judith E. et al, eds. *The Oxford Handbook of Childhood and Education in the Classical World*. New York: Oxford University Press, 2013.

Hamilton, Edith. *The Greek Way*. New York: W.W. Norton, 1993.

Hanson, Victor Davis. *The Wars of the Ancient Greeks and Their Invention of Western Military Culture*. London: Cassell, 2000.

Hanson, Victor Davis. *The Western Way of War: Infantry Battle in Classical Greece*. New York: University of California Press, 2009.

Hippocrates. *Hippocratic Writings*, trans. Francis Adams. Chicago: Encyclopedia Britannica, 1952.

James, Peter and Nick Thorpe. *Ancient Inventions*. New York: Ballantine, 2006.

Jenkins, Ian. *The Parthenon Frieze*. Austin: University of Texas, 2002.

Johnson, Paul. *Socrates: A Man for Our Times*. New York: Penguin, 2012.

Kagan, Donald. *The Peloponnesian War.* New York: Viking, 2003.

Karanika, Andromache. *Voices at Work: Women, Performance, and Labor in Ancient Greece.* Baltimore: Johns Hopkins University Press, 2014.

Lindberg David C. *The Beginnings of Western Science.* Chicago: University of Chicago Press, 2008.

MacLachlan, Bonnie. *Women in Ancient Greece: A Sourcebook.* New York: Bloomsbury Academic, 2012.

Martin, Thomas R. *Ancient Greece: From Prehistoric to Hellenistic Times.* New Haven: Yale University Press, 2013.

Matthew, Christopher. *A Storm of Spears: Understanding the Greek Hoplite at War.* South Yorkshire, Eng.: Pen & Sword, 2012.

Mikalson, Jon D. *Ancient Greek Religion.* New York: Wiley-Blackwell, 2009.

Morford, Mark P.O. and Robert J. Lenardon, *Classical Mythology.* New York: Oxford University Press, 2010.

Morris, Ian and Barry B. Powell. *The Greeks: History, Culture, and Society.* Old Tappan, NJ: Pearson, 2009.

Morrison, J.S. et al. *The Athenian Trireme: The History and Reconstruction of an Ancient Greek Warship.* New York: Cambridge University Press, 2000.

Ober, Josiah. *The Rise and Fall of Classical Greece.* Princeton: Princeton University Press, 2015.

Pedley, John G. *Greek Art and Archaeology.* New York: Prentice-Hall, 2011.

Pomeroy, Sarah B. et al. *Ancient Greece: A Political, Social, and Cultural History.* New York: Oxford University Press, 2011.

Rawson, Beryl, ed. *A Companion to Families in the Greek and Roman Worlds.* New York: Wiley-Blackwell, 2011.

Rodgers, Nigel. *The Illustrated Encyclopedia of Ancient Greece.* London: Lorenz, 2012.

Roy, Jim and Andre G. Roy. *Travel, Geography and Culture in Ancient Greece, Egypt and the Near East.* Leicester, Eng.: Oxbow, 2007.

Sarton, George. *Ancient Science Through the Golden Age of Greece.* New York: Dover, 2011.

Sekunda, Nicholas. *Marathon 490 BC.: The First Persian Invasion of Greece.* Oxford: Osprey, 2002.

Stansbury-O'Donnell, Mark D. *Looking at Greek Art.* New York: Cambridge University Press, 2010.

Swaddling, Judith. *The Ancient Olympic Games.* Austin: University of Texas Press, 2011.

Sweet, Waldo E., ed. *Sport and Recreation in Ancient Greece: A Sourcebook with Translations.* New York: Oxford University Press, 1987.

Taylor, A. E. *Aristotle.* New York: Dover, 2012.

Warner, Rex. *The Greek Philosophers.* New York: New American Library, 1958.

Warry, John. *Warfare in the Classical World.* New York: Barnes and Noble. 2005.

Wiedemann, Thomas, ed. *Greek & Roman Slavery.* London: Routledge, 2003.

Zimmern, Alfred Eckhard. *The Greek Commonwealth: Politics and Economics in Fifth-Century Athens.* Charleston, SC: Nabu Press, 2013.

About the Author

Classical historian and award-winning author Don Nardo has written numerous acclaimed volumes about ancient civilizations and peoples. They include studies of the histories, cultures, and mythologies of the Sumerians, Babylonians, Egyptians, Minoans, Greeks, Romans, Persians, Celts, and others. Nardo, who also composes and arranges orchestral music, lives with his wife Christine in Massachusetts.

INDEX